PREPARE
THE WAY

Daily Meditations for Advent

Imprimatur: ✠ Most Reverend Peter J. Jugis, JCD
                   Bishop of Charlotte
                   October 19, 2010

ISBN: 978-1-935302-70-4

Cover and interior design: Lauren A. Rupar

Cover Image: Detail, *The Annunciation*, Fra Filippo Lippi, Creative Commons

Printed and bound in the United States of America.

TAN Books
An Imprint of Saint Benedict Press, LLC
Charlotte, North Carolina
2012

PREPARE THE WAY

Daily Meditations for Advent

DR. RONALD THOMAS

Fra. Angelico, *Annunciation to M*

"Prepare the way of the Lord, make straight his paths."

With these familiar words, John the Baptist, the prophet sent by God to be the forerunner of the Messiah, issues the essential challenge of Advent.

But how can we, with our finite minds and sin-stained hearts, ever prepare a space within us adequate enough or worthy enough to receive a being as infinite in power and pure in goodness as our Lord and Savior, Jesus Christ?

We can cleanse our hearts from the stains of sin by repenting — through frequent confession, partaking of the Eucharist, giving alms and praying. And we can expand and nourish our minds through the power of words inspired by the Word, such as the meditations contained in this booklet.

With his daily meditations for Advent, Dr. Ron Thomas provides a 23-step path along which we can journey more deeply into Jesus' loving heart, and through which Jesus can travel more deeply into ours in return.

All we need to remember is that when we take our first halting steps toward Him, like the father in the parable of the prodigal son, He will run to us with His arms wide open. As Dr. Thomas writes, "The beauty of the generosity of God is that He will take anything we give Him. Any little thing. And He will receive it from us as if we had given Him everything."

May these daily meditations make your Advent abundantly fruitful, and your Christmas an especially blessed one!

Peter Paul Rubens, *The Great Last Judgment*

Sunday, December 2, 2012

FIRST SUNDAY IN ADVENT

In St. Matthew's Gospel, Jesus admonishes:

"Watch therefore, for you do not know on what day your Lord is coming. Therefore you also must be ready; for the Son of man is coming at an hour you do not expect." (24: 42, 44)

Advent brings about thoughts of the second coming of Christ, and in this, we recall Jesus' parable about the wheat and the tares. Remember that the wheat did not outgrow the tares. The harvest had to come, and then the tares were gathered up and burned.

So it is with evil in our world. At Christ's coming in great triumph on the last day, evil will then be destroyed—not before. There is no such thing as the progressive triumph of the Church over evil until a wonderful new world spontaneously generates. Progressivism is merely the vision of a Christ-less secularism, and the Church must be on its guard at all times against this sort of worldly, utopian fantasy. In our day, the fantasy proclaims that humanitarianism on a global scale, fueled by the requisite amount of money, will usher in a new age of peace and harmony.

Surely, these utopians underestimate the power of evil as it exists in the hearts of the most ostensibly benevolent persons. They also underestimate the glory, majesty, and justice of God against whom evil is an offense. Because it is God who is primarily offended, only He can "fix" the problem of evil. Those of us who believe in Christ adopt a godly strategy; we follow the word of the Lord. We wait for His coming triumph, and *we watch*!

Peter Paul Rubens, *The Miracle of St. Francis Xa*

DAY 2

Monday, December 3, 2012

ST. FRANCIS XAVIER

Advent is a good time to stop and consider the heroes of our faith who have actualized the Gospel. This is especially valuable in the case of the missionary Saints. Today is the feast of St. Francis Xavier, who died in 1552. He introduced the Faith in Japan and other locales in the Far East.

The death of St. Francis Xavier in the mission lands shows the arduous nature of the missionary task. Indeed, Jesus did call for us to abandon all and to follow Him, and a missionary who spends his life for the spread of the Gospel is a living sign that "neither death, nor life, nor angels, nor principalities, nor things present, nor things to come, nor powers, nor height, nor depth, nor anything else in all creation, will be able to separate us from the love of God in Christ Jesus our Lord." (Rom. 8: 38-39)

Advent is about the fullness of love coming down from Heaven. There is a mission vocation for each of us, even if it is not as dramatic as St. Francis Xavier's. There are plenty of pockets of darkness, sin, and spiritual ignorance in the circles in which we move day to day. The love of Jesus Christ drives out despair and death, and we are the ones who must proclaim an Almighty Love where we are.

St. Francis Xavier, pray for us, that we who live in a culture where the Gospel is everywhere present, but seldom believed and lived, may see it take root through the Catholic Faith!

DAY 3

Tuesday, December 4, 2012

Among the things we are waiting for this Advent is death.

Death is unavoidable. We wait for death every single day, whether we realize it or not. Mostly, we forget about it, which means that we do not consciously wait: we cover it over with many things—with anything—that might shield its horrid face from our sight.

Advent is a time in which the end of the world is expected—Jesus' promised return—but for most of us, the world will end in another way; we die. For most of us, Jesus' return to our sight will happen in this manner, even though we really hope for the *cosmic* event of His return.

The season of Advent reminds us that the coming of Christ is personal, always. It is never a take-it-or-leave-it proposition. More than anything Advent has to do with who and what will meet me in the end—be it at my death, or at the end of time.

Advent is so important for this very reason: we know that Christ has been born into the world, and that He plans to come again—but whether we live to see the coming Christmas or any Christmas thereafter is another matter. Advent is the time when we learn for certain that if death comes for us, it does not come alone. The Lord comes to meet us, as well. For Christians this is a marvelous hope and release. It is almost as if Easter comes in winter.

James Tissot, *The Miracle of the Loaves and F*

DAY 4

Wednesday, December 5, 2012

Here is a familiar story from St. Matthew's Gospel:

"Then Jesus called his disciples to him and said, 'I have compassion on the crowd, because they have been with me now three days, and have nothing to eat; and I am unwilling to send them away hungry, lest they faint on the way.'

"And the disciples said to him, 'Where are we to get bread enough in the desert to feed so great a crowd?'

"And Jesus said to them, 'How many loaves have you?' They said, 'Seven, and a few small fish.'" (Matthew 15: 32-34)

Every Gospel in the New Testament has an account of the miraculous feeding of the 5,000: the multiplication of loaves and fishes. St. Matthew and St. Mark have the additional account of the feeding of 4,000. There must be something crucial about this story. Catholics know that the Eucharist, easily celebrated more than 4,000 times each day in the world, is the key to the interpretation of these miraculous events. In fact, the Eucharistic feast, in which Jesus gives Himself, dwarfs the scope of these New Testament miracles. This is, of course, by Christ's own design.

Not only does the Eucharist reach far more people than even these wonderful New Testament events, it is of a high and ineffable character: it is Christ's own Body, Blood, Soul, and Divinity that is mediated in this miraculous sacrifice. With the feedings of the 4,000 and the 5,000, Jesus is merely preparing us for what is to come: the unending offering of the Eucharistic sacrifice all over the world. The most miraculous and astounding event that mankind can partake of is happening all around you—on every altar. Are you there to partake of it?

Hans Holbein d. J., *Madonna on a Th*

DAY 5

St. Nicholas

The original St. Nicholas, a fourth-century Bishop of Myra, in Asia Minor, was anything but the "jolly old elf" of "Twas the Night Before Christmas." In fact, he was a good deal better than that. He was a man of great conviction and great generosity. Fiercely opposed, equally, to heresy and to paganism, he could be as tender as a lamb to those who lacked the necessities of life, to children, and to women in danger of being pressed into prostitution. He was also a man of genuine miracle, not mere magic. Countless miracles have been attributed to his intercession.

The Gospel reading for the day is from St. Luke, in which Jesus says to the disciples "behold, I send you out as lambs in the midst of wolves. Carry no purse, no bag, no sandals; and salute no one on the road." All of this reminds us of St. Nicholas' lack of concern for money. He held the material things in this life cheap, and the life to come very dear. He understood what money was good for: the love and purposes of God, not excess or the effort to buy love.

Among the representations of Saints in Christian art, the images of St. Nicholas and the Virgin Mary are the two most common. That is understandable, for the Virgin Mary and Nicholas, together, represent completely what is important in this season of Advent as it competes with our premature Christmas, namely, giving is far better than receiving, and the best gifts are the ones that come from God himself.

ST. AMBROSE

MILAN

SAINT

Icon, *Saint Ambrose and Saint Pat*

DAY 6

Friday, December 7, 2012

St. Ambrose

In the Gospel of St. Matthew, Jesus asks, "What do you think? If a man has one hundred sheep and one of them has gone astray, does he not leave the ninety-nine on the mountains and go in search of the one that went astray?" (Mt. 18:12)

This is a startling Advent image that depicts God coming to us like a good Shepherd in search of one lost sheep. God's coming to us is personal and intimate.

The contrast between His care, His effort and our pitiful condition should reinforce how undeserving we are of so great a love. He cares for us in ways we hardly care for ourselves, much less for others. Only He sees what is true and valuable in the world and its people. Only He notices when and how a sheep has gone astray.

There once was a man, a very gifted man, who had lost his way spiritually, despite the efforts of his saintly mother to point him in the right direction. Jesus can use His faithful servants to go find a lost sheep, to be a good shepherd in His stead, and in this case He did. The faithful servant went, found the sheep, poured the healing balm of Sacred Scripture on his soul, and brought him to the waters of Baptism. That shepherd was St. Ambrose, bishop of Milan in the late fourth century. The sheep was a man named Augustine, before he became St. Augustine, and, of course, the saintly mother was St. Monica. Today the universal Church remembers St. Ambrose, the faithful shepherd. He went and searched; he found and reconciled a lost sheep. He is a great Advent saint, whose actions reflect God's coming to us.

Bartolomé Esteban Perez Murillo, *The Annunci*

DAY 7

Saturday, December 8, 2012

IMMACULATE CONCEPTION

When it is suggested that Mary is at the pinnacle of the history of Israel, sometimes people object. They say, "Jesus Christ is at the summit of that covenant history." This sounds like a robust defense of the place of Christ, but it is actually a mistaken opinion. Jesus Christ is the very giver of the covenant: the covenant does not produce Him. He is God; and, this, the Jewish covenant tradition never could have envisioned. Jesus Christ transmutes the covenant with Israel into the universal covenant in His Blood, leading to eternal life, a new Heaven and a new Earth.

Mary, on the other hand, is the one mere mortal in that Old Covenant whose total being is pleasing to God and who may serve as the portal for His Incarnation. She is pleasing to God by God's own design, of course, especially in her holy and Immaculate Conception. She is superior to the other miraculous mothers: Sarah, Hannah, and Elizabeth—and she is bound up in the purposes of God more immediately than all the patriarchs: Moses, Isaac, Jacob, and even Abraham himself, for Mary is the second Eve, and there is no role higher than that, outside of a second Adam, which is Christ—and to Him, Mary gives birth.

Ah, the power of the paradoxes of God. Behold! The dwelling of God is with men, and all things are made new. *God* brings freedom for captive man and tramples down death by death.

Truly, Israel's rose has blossomed, and God has dwelt among us. Why will all generations call Mary blessed? Because Jesus Christ is born of Mary, born for us, His lowly servants!

Bartholomeus Breenbergh, *The Preaching of John the Ba*

DAY 8

Second Sunday in Advent

The traditional hymn, "On Jordan's Bank," features the familiar figure of John the Baptist, the voice crying in the wilderness:

On Jordan's bank the Baptist's cry
announces that the Lord is nigh;
awake and hearken, for he brings
glad tidings of the King of kings.

Then cleansed be every breast from sin;
make straight the way for God within,
prepare we in our hearts a home
where such a mighty Guest may come.

For thou art our salvation, Lord,
our refuge and our great reward;
without thy grace we waste away
like flowers that wither and decay.

To heal the sick stretch out thine hand,
and bid the fallen sinner stand;
shine forth and let thy light restore
Earth's own true loveliness once more.

All praise, eternal Son, to thee,
whose advent doth thy people free;
whom with the Father we adore
and Holy Ghost for evermore.

All of the words of this classic hymn speak to our essential tasks this Advent: to prepare our hearts, to accept God's grace, to dismiss the resistance and contrariness and distraction, to greet the lovely advent of salvation with joy and cries of deliverance.

The life of John the Baptist was dedicated to this Advent of redemption and release. You and I have the realization of this promise in full. Christ Himself has prepared His royal highway in our hearts. We should "awake and hearken" and stand to greet Him when He comes.

Aldo Locatelli, *Judgement and scenes from the Day of W*
Church of San Pellegr

Monday, December 10, 2012

What does Christ get out of you?

You may be shocked by the reversal implied in this question. We usually think of what we shall get out of Him!

Or, maybe you're scandalized that Christ should be spoken of as someone who needs something or as someone "on the make," as they say.

But it isn't impious to ask this question, for you cannot exist without Him for a moment. He made you from nothing. His glory is more excellent than the whole of creation rolled up in a ball. His justice is impeccable. From Him all things come; to Him everything is due. All things that exist owe Him their homage; to Him they must return their very selves.

So then, the question: What does Christ get out of you?

Let's put the matter concretely:

Can Christ depend on you today for some aspect of His work in the world? Can He expect you to share His love in some place or with some person, right where He wants it? Can He count on you to speak His truth in some context to someone? When the sun sets on this day will He find that you belong more to Him permanently than you did when the day began?

The one who is coming to meet us as our Judge—something we stress in this Advent season—requires of us the entirety of our lives. The good news is that if we can make this offering, He will give us something of greater value than our lives. He will give us *His life*—forever—which is more of a gift than we will ever give Him.

Paolo de Matt

DAY 10

Tuesday, December 11, 2012

St. Matthew's Gospel relates the parable of two sons being sent into the vineyard. One does the will of his father; the other just says that he will serve! It is a parable about real discipleship and obedience to God.

The Blessed Virgin Mary has always been held up to us as a model of discipleship and obedience to God. And we always have need of being refreshed by that model. We lose our way so easily, and go our own way so thoughtlessly. We lose the belief that in obedience is the freedom, and in submission is the victory. In short, we forget the purposes of God, and our vineyard becomes a tangled mess.

How much better it is, each day, to clear and order a patch of the vineyard for the purposes of God. Very few of us can say yes to God as completely as Mary. It is enough for most of us to stake just a bit each day upon the purposes of God. But oh, how far we do come, just doing that.

The beauty of the generosity of God is that He will take anything we give Him. Any little thing. And He will receive it from us as if we had given Him everything. Imagine the Maker of All having the heart to receive, with real and unbounded gratitude, what poor returns we offer Him. It sounds like the God who saved the world by the gift of one tiny Baby. It sounds like the God who seeks the one lost sheep, heedless of the ninety-nine. It sounds like *our* God, whose mercy is without end.

Fra Angelico, *The Gates of He*

Wednesday, December 12, 2012

The ancient plainchant *Rorate Coeli* is traditional during Advent:

> *Rorate coeli desuper et nubes pluant justum,*
> *Aperiatur terra et germinet salvatorem*

Translated, it reads:

> *Drop down dew, ye heavens, from above, and let the clouds rain the just,*
> *Let the earth be opened and send forth a Saviour.*

The text of this hauntingly beautiful chant is from Isaiah, Chapter 45. It expresses the hope of the Old Covenant for its Messiah, a longing of many centuries eventually fulfilled in Christ Jesus.

Longing and hope are key aspects of Advent that we share with those who lived before the birth of the Lord. The key difference is that we are waiting for what we know, our joy is ecstatic and complete, our bodies rest in hope, our souls are filled.

From above and below, God has come to meet us. The heavens have sent Him and the Earth yields Him up to us. The reign of God has begun.

When this present world has given way to the fullness of the Kingdom of God and Christ returns, never to depart, Heaven and Earth will be more beautiful and more holy than even this lovely musical token of our faith. It seems unlikely, but it is nonetheless true.

Until that time, we will praise, and hope, and anticipate with the most beautiful things that the Tradition of the Church has given us. Things like chant and the noble ecclesiastical Latin.

> *Drop down dew, ye heavens, from above, and let the clouds rain the just,*
> *Let the earth be opened and send forth a Saviour.*

Giovanni Battista Tiepolo, *The Communion of Saint*

DAY 12

Thursday, December 13, 2012

St. Lucy

Dante, the great Italian poet and author of *The Divine Comedy*, studied philosophy so intently over the course of two years that his eyes were dangerously injured. This is not a warning against the study of philosophy. On the contrary, it is a lesson about a great Saint whose feast day we observe today.

For healing, Dante asked the intercession of St. Lucy, an early fourth century Italian martyr. St. Lucy (or Lucia) has a name with a connection to the Latin word *lux* or light. This is very ironic, for when she was persecuted for being a Christian, her eyes were gouged out.

The light of Lucy's eyes was put to an end, but not the light of her eternal reward. She is now the celebrated patroness of all those who suffer diseases of the eye. Perhaps you have even heard her name in the Roman Canon, or Eucharistic prayer I, of the Mass.

In Scandinavia, where the daylight this time of year is almost unbearably short and the nights longer than ever, St. Lucy's Day is a celebration of the light that never fades, Jesus Christ. Young girls don white dresses, a red sash for martyrdom, and lighted candle-crowns in honor of the light-bearing Saint.

Dante's eyes were, in fact, healed, and his devotion to St. Lucy cemented for a lifetime. She even appears in *The Divine Comedy*, depicted as one who aids the poet in his journey of spiritual illumination. St. Lucy and all the Saints work tirelessly on our behalf. We should approach them with our requests, confident in their care for us. More than anything, they are part of the grace that will lead us to Heaven where we shall gaze upon the one, true light, forever.

Johann Michael Rottmayr, *Allegory of*

DAY 13

G. K. Chesterton once said that, for unbelievers, any stick is good enough to beat Christianity with. Some think the Faith too stringent; others think it too loose. Some think it too hard, some think it too soft.

If people can attack the Faith from every side, Chesterton asserts, perhaps it is because it is just right. Perhaps it is just what it ought to be. The problem then, is not with the Faith, but with people. Their expectations are for something that suits them; not for something that will tell them an unwelcomed truth.

Jesus marvels at the people of His day. They don't seem to want anything that God wants for them. God sends John the Baptist—he is too strict. God sends Jesus himself—but He is too unconventional. Jesus strongly suggests that they are like fickle children.

We who believe would like to think we know God's purposes and follow them rightly. But is there something this day that God intends for us that we are resisting, rationalizing away, or rejecting?

There is simply nothing related to the life of faith that is more important than participating—willingly and obediently—in God's purposes as He makes them known to us. We who believe must not be fickle children, but obedient sons and daughters, gaining eternal life through participation with the only One who can grant it.

Murillo, *The Holy Family with the Infant Sa*

Saturday, December 15, 2012

One of the most important aspects of our keeping of Advent relates to the way in which the coming of Christ fulfills the Old Covenant that God made with Israel.

For instance, Elijah is expected before the coming of the Messiah. This inspired image communicates the truth that the Messiah will perfectly fulfill all that the prophets foretold and all that they stood for. Elijah will come and declare it to be so.

Indeed Elijah does appear, with Moses, on the Mount of Transfiguration, but this is to the small, select group of Peter, James, and John.

Our Lord, however, would give us to believe that the *public* face of Elijah in this, the time of his coming, is, in fact, John the Baptist.

John the Baptist is the prophet's prophet—and he is the *last* prophet of the Advent of Christ.

No other prophet was privileged to see the very face of the Messiah he heralded. John alone has this honor: John, in his camel's hair and with his strange and spare diet.

If we want to see how the Old Covenant is fulfilled in the new, we should look at John the Baptist. He sees the sunrise of the new Kingdom in his own time. So do we, in this Advent season.

Alexander Andreyevich Ivanov, *John the Ba*

DAY 15

Sunday, December 16, 2012

THIRD SUNDAY IN ADVENT

In St. Matthew's Gospel, we encounter a passage where John the Baptist languishes in prison and wonders if he was right to make all those large claims about the love of God visible in Jesus of Nazareth! Through his followers he asks of Jesus, pitifully: "Are you the one who is to come or are we to await another?"

Jesus answers John: "Go tell John all that I am doing: the healing of the blind, deaf, lame and possessed." And Jesus adds a curious finish to His answer, "Tell John, blessed is the one who takes no offense at me."

Jesus summons John to use his eyes of faith to see God's love and power in all that Jesus is doing. He bids John to look past his prison and see the dawning of the age that God had promised through the prophets—to rejoice, even though he has been cut off and cast into the shadows.

Advent reminds us that just like John the Baptist, we might not grasp God's love in Jesus. Instead, we might recoil in dismay at all the things that assault us: the trials, and the senseless indignities that wound us.

But this darkness, too, is part of the promise: a time to know God better, to lean wholly upon Him and not upon the usual supports. Advent, indeed the whole course of our life, is a time of waiting and watching—and blessed is he who does not take offense at God's methods and manner. In pondering the mystery of God's coming to us, let us understand that those times when God seems distant and unknowable are but the way He heralds a sunrise for our hearts.

Jacopo Pontormo, *Mary Embraces St. Eliza*

DAY 16

Monday, December 17, 2012

The first Christmas was a matter of intense waiting. Consider the time between now and Christmas from the vantage point of the Blessed Virgin Mary. For her, nine months of puzzlement and wonder fill the space from the Annunciation to the Birth. As the Birth draws closer, she wonders: Will God deliver on His promises, despite the attitude of those around me?

Are you able to believe that in the very midst of this world, God has begun a revolution of unrestricted power? You already know the paradox of the Babe: all that power in all that weakness. Truly God's ways are not our ways.

Isn't it odd, but very significant, that all the nations of the world are still waiting upon the things they all hold out as promises: justice, human dignity, peace?

The world does not know what it is waiting for, but we do. We will wait on what God is doing, and we will rejoice, now, on behalf of a world that has nothing to rejoice in.

The poet Rainer Maria Rilke once wrote to a young poet both of Christ and of this young poet's life. He asked quite poetically:

"What keeps you from projecting His birth into times that are in the process of becoming, and living your life like a painful and beautiful day in the history of a great gestation?"

The "great gestation" of God, known by Our Lady Mary, and every one of the Baptized who wait in hope, is achieving fullness--it will not be long now. It is not long until hope clothes itself in flesh and we turn and see it together.

Nicolas Poussin, *Adoration of the Shep*

Tuesday, December 18, 2012

Gloria in excelsis Deo. Glory to God in the highest—so goes the first line of the angelic hymn that has become a permanent part of the Liturgy.

But did not Jesus Christ come down to us? Didn't He lay aside the form of His heavenly glory to come among us?

To express this fact, G. K. Chesterton penned a famous poem entitled "*Gloria in Profundis*," or "Glory to God in the Lowest."

Low, indeed, is the estate that Jesus chooses: a stable-cave in Bethlehem, the smallness and poverty of human infancy. So Chesterton writes:

There has fallen on earth for a token
A god too great for the sky.
He has burst out of all things and broken
The bounds of eternity:
Into time and the terminal land
He has strayed like a thief or a lover,
For the wine of the world brims over,
Its splendor is spilt on the sand.

Who is proud when the heavens are humble,
Who mounts if the mountains fall,
If the fixed suns topple and tumble
And a deluge of love drowns all—
Who rears up his head for a crown

Who holds up his will for a warrant
Who strives with the starry torrent
When all that is good goes down?

Indeed, we are waiting for all that is good to come down to us. It will come. *He* will come.

And so, continuing with Chesterton, we say:

Glory to God in the Lowest
The spout of the stars in spate—
Where thunderbolt thinks to be slowest
And the lightning fears to be late:
As men dive for sunken gem
Pursuing, we hunt and hound it,
The fallen star has found it .
In the Cavern of Bethlehem.

Rogier van der Weyden, *The Naming of John the B...*

DAY 18

Wednesday, December 19, 2012

"Thus says the Lord God: Lo, I am sending my messenger to prepare the way for me. . . " (Malachi 3:1)

Consider how the Herald of the Lord, John the Baptist, enters the world. Eight days after John is born, when he is circumcised and named, his father, Zechariah, finally regains his speech. His tongue is loosed for praise and the blessing of God. He has been mute since the time of his interrogation of the Angel who brought the news of this extraordinary child.

The people who witness this marvel ask themselves, "What, then, will this child be?" Zechariah answers the question in the famous canticle we call the *Benedictus*:

> *Blessed be the Lord God of Israel;*
> *for he hath visited and redeemed his people.*
> *And hath raised up a mighty salvation for us,*
> *in the house of his servant David.*
> *. . . And thou, child, shalt be called the prophet of the Highest;*
> *for thou shalt go before the face of the Lord to prepare his ways,*
> *To give knowledge of salvation unto his people, for the remission of their sins.*

John will "prepare the way" by urging everyone to repentance and proclaim Jesus as the "Lamb of God" in the sight of all. His role having been fulfilled, he willingly recedes into the background to allow the "Day-spring from on high" to shine upon all. After his miraculous birth and all of his strenuous and heroic actions, John receives a final gift of humility—and of peace. We, too, should be waiting in humility and quiet confidence. The dawn is near. We have cleansed ourselves in preparation by repenting of our sins. God will visit and redeem His people very soon.

Domenico Beccafumi, *Proclam*

Thursday, December 20, 2012

In St. Luke's Gospel we read:

"In the sixth month the angel Gabriel was sent from God to a city of Galilee named Nazareth, to a virgin betrothed to a man whose name was Joseph, of the house of David; and the virgin's name was Mary. . . And Mary said, 'Behold, I am the handmaid of the Lord; let it be to me according to your word.' And the angel departed from her." (1:26-27, 38)

It is significant that Mary, who consents to have this holy child of the Holy Spirit, is herself, not much more than a child. She could have been only thirteen or so when she was betrothed to Joseph of Nazareth. But herein lies her appeal to us. Her childlikeness is the childlikeness that God had envisioned all along for Israel. She simply holds out her hand to be led, and says: "Behold, I am the handmaid of the Lord; let it be to me according to your word."

She is the perfect daughter of Israel: if it is the will of the Lord that such a strange thing happen, so be it.

People often remark about how Jesus, the Savior of the world, was born in a backwater of the Roman Empire as a peasant. The impression is heightened if one remembers also that this was not even a very significant time in Israel's history. Still, there is at no other time in Israel's history obedience like Mary's. It should give us pause to wonder. God has wrested His will for Israel out of the time of its very humiliation. *Mary* is the name Israel bears when it obeys God and places itself as the willing handmaid of the Lord.

Giotto di Bondone, *The Visitation*

DAY 20

Friday, December 21, 2012

St. Luke writes:

"In those days Mary arose and went with haste into the hill country, to a city of Judah, and she entered the house of Zechariah and greeted Elizabeth. And when Elizabeth heard the greeting of Mary, the babe leaped in her womb; and Elizabeth was filled with the Holy Spirit, and she exclaimed with a loud cry, 'Blessed are you among women, and blessed is the fruit of your womb! And why is this granted me, that the mother of my Lord should come to me?'" (1: 39-43)

The story of the Visitation of Mary to her cousin Elizabeth is so familiar to us. Elizabeth blesses Mary for her fidelity and courage. John the Baptist adds his salute from within the womb, leaping at the voice of the Mother of God.

In the presence of the Mother of God, we are moved to excitement and blessing. This Blessed Mother, the portal for the divine life entering into the world, is a constant companion for us, always carrying within herself the reality of her Son. Indeed, her divine Son has placed Himself in her womb and in her safekeeping *for our sake*. We are intended to know Jesus through Mary and rejoice in the fact that in Mary's flesh as well as in His own, Our Lord has hallowed and sanctified our lot as human beings. This is great news of salvation. It is close to us, and it is personal. The Blessed Mother's presence among us reminds us of this, constantly.

Fransois Vanden Pitte, *Mary Queen of He*

Saturday, December 22, 2012

Today in the readings for Mass, we hear of the encounter between Elizabeth and the Virgin Mary, and we get the marvelous song of Mary called the *Magnificat*:

> *My soul doth magnify the Lord and my spirit hath rejoiced in God my Saviour*
> *For he hath regarded the low estate of his handmaiden*
> *For behold from henceforth all generations shall call me blessed*

Reciting the *Magnificat*, as we do daily in the evening office, one gains hope that, truly, God will do all that He has said He will do in this world, and that each one of us is part of the people through whom God will do it!

Being the Church is never so exciting as when hope creeps in and one comes to understand whose order will ultimately prevail—God's!

> *He hath showed strength with his arm,*
> *He hath scattered the proud in the imagination of their hearts . . .*

God's victory and promise are as real as a child in the womb, as potent as the raising of a Jewish girl from obscurity to the place of a Queen.

When Elizabeth greeted Mary she said, "Blessed are you, Mary, because you have believed that there would be a fulfillment of what was spoken to you by the Lord."

And blessed are we when we come to believe and trust in this same way.

Mary became a Queen, not just Queen for a day, but a Queen as long as the promise of God is believed, and among all who claim it, indeed, as long as her Son shall reign.

Therefore, we ask for Mary's prayers, that we might know her Son as she knew Him—without complication, simply, and intimately.

Anton Raphael Mengs, *The Dream of Saint Jo*

DAY 22

Sunday, December 23, 2012

FOURTH SUNDAY IN ADVENT

St. Matthew's Gospel relates the story of how Joseph learns that Mary's pregnancy is of God:

"Behold, an angel of the Lord appeared to [Joseph] in a dream, saying, 'Joseph, son of David, do not fear to take Mary your wife, for that which is conceived in her is of the Holy Spirit.'" (Mt. 1: 20)

Compared to the Holy Virgin, Joseph's role in the history of salvation is indirect, and when the Angel of the Lord makes his pronouncement to him, it is to a man of great honor, but also of great fear and weakness.

St. Joseph's role is just like the role most men play in the lives of their wives and children: they protect, they provide, they deliberate concerning the welfare of the family, and they toil under the conditions of working life. It is very true that a husband and father, sometimes more visibly than anyone, is responsible for the decisions he makes.

An Angel of the Lord clarifies to Joseph, this special father and guardian, the precise nature of Mary's pregnancy and that under the power of the Holy Spirit, he should engage the powers of his manhood for a supremely important task.

Even before the special child is born, Joseph must embrace Mary as a beloved, care for her, and venerate her not only as his spouse, but as the spouse of the Holy Spirit.

Being a father, and a husband, and a man is not always easy, but St. Joseph shows that God will indeed use a man who with honor and courage will obey. St. Joseph, pray for us!

Correggio, *Holy Ni*

Monday, December 24, 2012

The journey of Advent is nearly complete. Something has been building, waiting to be born—a type of freedom—as Charles Wesley's hymn intones:

Come, thou long-expected Jesus,
born to set thy people free;
from our fears and sins release us,
let us find our rest in thee.

Israel's strength and consolation,
hope of all the earth thou art:
dear desire of every nation,
joy of every longing heart.

"Every nation" is to be delivered: the whole Earth and every heart in it. This is a tremendous mystery. More mysterious still will be the mode in which our deliverance comes, and so the hymn continues:

Born thy people to deliver,
born a child, and yet a king,
born to reign in us for ever,
now thy gracious kingdom bring.

By thine own eternal Spirit
rule in all our hearts alone;
by thine all-sufficient merit
raise us to thy glorious throne.

The Child born into our world will change everything. This tiny King is our route to a throne and a Kingdom. The news is too great, too good, too large to take in. God knows this, which is why He chose to come among us in the humility of infancy and what seemed to be powerlessness.

When will this world rise to bless its King? When will it honor its Lord and maker? When will it wake up to its destiny and its Savior? The little Baby of Bethlehem is a shock and a surprise. The coming of Christ again in power and great triumph will also be a shock, but a wonderful and long-awaited fulfillment for all of those who have honored their King during their earthly pilgrimage.

Come, thou long-expected Jesus!

Reference

Works of art in this publication were taken from Wikimedia Commons and are considered public domain with the exception of those that require photographer notation.

Intro. *Annunciation to Mary*, Fra. Angelico (1430-1432)

Day 1 *The Great Last Judgement*, Peter Paul Rubens (1617)

Day 2 *The Miracle of St. Francis Xavier*, Peter Paul Ruben (1619-1620)

Day 3 *The Poem of the Soul — Memory of Heaven*, Anne-Francois-Louis Janmot

Day 4 *The Miracle of the Loaves and Fishes*, James Tissot (1885-1896)

Day 5 *Madonna on a Throne*, Hans Holbein d. J.

Day 6 *St. Ambrose and St. Patrick*, Icon

Day 7 *The Annunciation*, Bartolomé Esteban Perez Murillo (1655-1660)

Day 8 *The Preaching of John the Baptist*, Bartholomeus Breenbergh (1634)

Day 9 *Judgement and scenes from the Day of Wrath*, Church of San Pellegrino, Aldo Locatelli (1948-1958). Photo: Ricardo André Frantz

Day 10 *The Annunciation*, Paolo de Matteis (1712)

Day 11 *The Gates of Heaven*, Fra Angelico

Day 12 *The Communion of Saint Lucy*, Giovanni Battista Tiepolo (1746)

Day 13 *Allegory of Faith*, St. Charles Church of Vienna, Johann Michael Rottmayr (1714), Photo: Wolfgang Sauber

Day 14 *The Holy Family with the Infant Saint John*, Bartolomé Esteban Perez Murillo (1655-1660)

Day 15 *John the Baptist*, Alexander Andreyevich Ivanov (1824)

Day 16 *Mary Embraces St. Elizabeth*, Jacopo Pontormo (1528-1529)

Day 17 *Adoration of the Shepherds*, Nicolas Poussin

Day 18 *The Naming of John the Baptist*, Rogier van der Weyden

Day 19 *Proclamation*, Domenico Beccafumi (1545-1546)

Day 20 *The Visitation*, Giotto di Bondone (1306)

Day 21 *Mary Queen of Heaven*, Fransois Vanden Pitte (1485-1500)

Day 22 *The Dream of Saint Joseph*, Anton Raphael Mengs (1773)

Day 23 *Holy Night*, Correggio (1528-1530)

Dr. Ronald Thomas is Assistant Professor of Theology at Belmont Abbey College. Before he was received into the Catholic Church, he served as an Episcopal priest for thirteen years and as a Methodist minister for five years prior to that.

Before coming to Belmont Abbey, Dr. Thomas taught at Christian Brothers University, Crichton College, the University of Mississippi, and Rhodes College.

He received his Ph.D. in Theology from the University of Cambridge (England) and his Master of Divinity at the Candler School of Theology at Emory University (Atlanta, GA). He was also a student of Theology at the University of Goettingen (Germany). He earned his B.A. in Philosophy and Psychology at The University of Memphis (Memphis, TN).

Dr. Thomas' wife, Sally Thomas, is a writer and a frequent contributor to *First Things* magazine, an influential intellectual journal. The Thomases have four children and live in Lincolnton, North Carolina.

The Perfect Holy Hour
Meditation during Lent!

Originally published in 1935, this volume offers a variety of spiritual counsels and reflections, arranged on a framework of the phrases of the *Our Father* and giving special attention to the sufferings of Our Lord in His Passion.

A wide-ranging treatment, perfect for visits to the Blessed Sacrament, prayers after Mass and daily meditation. This book touches on the topics of sin, divine love, suffering, justice, forgiveness, and many more, concluding each topic with an original prayer. Plus, it is embellished with a generous selection of pious verses and traditional Catholic prayers.

Also included are John Cardinal Newman's powerful meditation on the "Mental Sufferings of Our Lord in His Passion," as well as a paraphrase of the *Our Father* by St. Francis of Assisi and another paraphrase from the *Divine Comedy* of Dante.

The Our Father in Gethsemane
$7.95   ISBN: 9780895552648

Order Now at
TANBooks.com!